BIBL

FOR

HOMOSEXUAL MARRIAGE

A MESSAGE FOR
THE BRIDE OF CHRIST

A Riddle Challenges a Bible Believing
Church To Take a Deeper Look

William J Meiners

Biblical Support for Homosexual Marriage /
A Message for the Bride of Christ

Author: William J. Meiners

Publisher: Dominicus Group
Suite 200, 601 Kewanna
Jeffersonville, IN 47130

LCCN: 2012937003
ISBN: 978-1470195700

1 2 3 4 5 6 7 8 9 CS 16 15 14 13 12

Dedication

This book is dedicated to:
All those who have not yet experienced
God's Perfect Love
and to
The Bride of Christ

Acknowledgments

To the saints of old
who have gone before,
whose work
the saints of today
have grown by
and whose shoulders
we stand upon

CONTENTS

THE RIDDLE

There Are Two Couples:

The first couple is as perfect as imaginable. This couple loves God, their children, each other, the world, and even their enemies just about as perfectly as humanly possible. They love just like Jesus.

The second couple is exactly identical to the first couple. Their love for God, each other, the world, etc. is exactly the same as the first couple. The only difference between the couples is that the first couple is male/female and the second couple is either "both male" or "both female." Other than their sexual orientation everything else is identical. They also love just like Jesus.

IT IS WRITTEN

IN

THE

BEGINNING

?

The Riddle Is:

According to the Bible, would their judgments when they stand before God to give an account be:

A. **"Identical"**, since 1st Samuel 16:7 says the Lord looks upon the heart and not on the outward appearance.

OR

B. **"Different"**, since Leviticus 18:23 says man lying with man is an abomination.

IT IS WRITTEN

WAS

THE

WORD

JOHN 1:1 (KJV)

1

THE STORY
BEHIND THE RIDDLE

It was a Wednesday night. I was attending a service at my church when it happened. A thought came. A thought that I wished would not have come. Then again I did not want to prevent it from coming either, if in actuality the source and originator was God. That was a big "If." Nevertheless the thought had come and there was not an option whereby I could send it back. What caused my apprehension was not the thought but what came with it, a "choice." I had the option of choosing between a *"rock"* or a *"hard place"*, and I had five minutes to decide. If I did not choose the *"rock"* my choice would automatically default to the *"hard place."*

AND THE

WORD

WAS WITH

GOD

JUST MAKE IT A LITTLE CLEARER

Don't you love God. *"Just make it a little clearer which way you want me to go and I will gladly choose that option."* Have you ever said that to God? I have many times. I have learned though that God is not going to speak louder. If I want to hear clearer I have always found it requires me to die more to self and to my other distractions.

FULLY DEAD NOW

I have thought many times, *"Well, I believe I am fully dead now. I shouldn't have a problem clearly hearing God's voice from now on."* After many years I have finally come to the conclusion it is going to be a while. What I have discovered is that God knows perfectly well how loud He needs to speak in order for me to hear. I have this feeling that God believes by lowering His voice when our hearing improves, it gives us the opportunity to grow even more. I believe He thinks that He is being a good father that way. The more I grow the more sure I am though that God is not only a good Father but a perfect Father with a perfect love for us.

Here was the rock choice:
After the service tell the riddle to the pastor and the elders.

AND THE

WORD

WAS

GOD

Here was the hard place choice:
Keep silent, do not say anything, ignore the thought, or wait till another time.

CHOOSING CORRECTLY

Experience had taught me that sometimes God is in the rock choice and sometimes God is in the hard place. Many times *"choosing correctly"* results in being more blessed in our present situation and life but not always. However *"choosing incorrectly"* seems to almost always result in a decrease in sensing God's presence and with God seeming more at a distance, at least temporarily. This can be a huge downer especially if you are use to experiencing a close and sensitive relationship with God.

DIEING TO FEAR

Well, I decided to die to my fears and be obedient to what I sensed the Spirit of God was leading me to do. After the service I told the pastor what I felt and shared the riddle with him and the elders who were present. I then left them to decide what it meant and how to interpret it.

AWARE OF POTENTIAL CONSEQUENCES

I was fully aware of the churches policy on homosexual marriage and I knew that the riddle might

THE SAME

WAS IN THE

BEGINNING

WITH

GOD

not be received well. I was hoping though that God was going to guide the pastor and elders to take a deeper look at the churches position on the subject.

PASTOR'S & ELDERS' RESPONSE

What was the pastor's and the elders' response? I was immediately removed from teaching Sunday school. I was shunned and silenced by the leaders of my home fellowship group. I was eventually asked to leave the church and not to set foot again on the church campus.

REWARDS FOR GETTING IT RIGHT

There is absolutely no question that it can be a challenge to hear and be obedient to the promptings of the Holy Spirit. The rewards are great however when you do hear correctly and respond appropriately. When God truly leads you to do something that stretches you and you obey, there is almost always such a keen awareness of God in your spirit that even if the whole world seems to be against you, it doesn't really matter to you. In fact you actually have empathy and sadness for those who may be persecuting you.

HINDRANCES TO HEARING

The two biggest hindrances to hearing the voice of the Holy Spirit I have found are 1) Pride and 2) Not obeying or following the promptings of the Holy Spirit

ALL

THINGS

WERE MADE BY

HIM

JOHN 1:3 (KJV)

when you receive them. Timing also can be very important in many instances especially as one grows in spiritual maturity and depth.

FALSE LEADINGS NOT FROM GOD

Evil spiritual influences and thoughts are consistently trying to imitate the Holy Spirit and lead us in wrong directions and into destructive actions and decisions. Hindsight gives the clearest insight but that doesn't help at the time you need to make the decision.

Even with my church's negative reaction and consequences, I am so glad that I was obedient in following the witness in my spirit on that occasion. It has led to so many blessings as well as a richer and deeper insight and relationship with God.

NOT WHAT GOD WANTS

Everything that happens in this world and in God's church are not necessarily what God wants or what He desires to happen. When it became clear that the riddle had been taken by the pastor and the elders as a threat and attack on themselves and the Bible instead of a help, it motivated me to do a biblical exegesis on the topic.

That exegesis has led to the writing of this book.

AND

WITHOUT

HIM

2

WHY
A CORRECT UNDERSTANDING
IS IMPORTANT

If the main mission of the church is to draw people to God, how important is it for the Christian church to get this issue correct?

RENDERING THE CHURCH INEFFECTIVE

Being wrong saps the Christian church of its' power and credibility as well as its effectiveness to share the good news of Jesus Christ and free people in bondage. Great condemnation is being heaped upon the church because of its stance on homosexual marriage. I believe in standing for truth even if it is unpopular. However it is very important to make sure that the biblical truth we are standing up for is truly biblical. Otherwise it is a lose-lose situation.

IT IS WRITTEN

WAS NOT

ANY THING MADE

THAT WAS MADE

CHRISTIANS BEING PERCEIVED
AS OUT OF TOUCH WITH GOD

The percentage of people who see allowing homosexual marriage as the right thing to do is very high and is growing. To someone who is not trying to follow biblical and religious guidelines and is a loving and open-minded person, it can be quite natural and easy to believe that there is nothing wrong with allowing homosexuals to marry. They then discount the Christian church and see it as out of touch with God. The result of which is that many get steered away from the truth of the gospel of Jesus Christ and the Bible.

ON THE SURFACE

I can understand why many Christians believe that homosexual marriage is sin. On the surface, the Bible does seem to clearly say that homosexuality is sin in the eyes of God. In addition, traditionally homosexuality has always been looked down upon both in society as well as in the church.

HAVING NOBLE CHARACTER AND
SEARCHING THE SCRIPTURES REQUIRED

Jesus told the great Bible scholars of His time who "thought" they knew the Bible scriptures better than others that they were blind to what the scriptures were

IN HIM

WAS

LIFE

really saying. (Matthew 23:16) The Bible says that the Jews of Berea were more noble then the Jews of Thessalonica and searched the scriptures daily whether the things Paul and Silas were saying were so. (Acts 17:11) If you are a Christian that truly wants to be a part of accomplishing the commission Jesus Christ gave the church, then I hope you are willing to look a little deeper in the Bible to make sure your position on homosexual marriage is correct.

AND

THE LIFE

WAS

THE LIGHT

OF MEN

3

MILK AND SOLID FOOD

The apostle Paul wrote to the church in Corinth:
"And I, brethren, could not speak to you as to spiritual people but as to carnal, as to babes in Christ. <u>I fed you with milk and not with solid food; for until now you were not able to receive it</u>, and even now you are still not able; 1 Corinthians 3:1,2 (NKJV)

And Paul's letter to the Hebrews:
For though <u>by this time you ought to be teachers</u>, you need someone to teach you again the first principles of the oracles of God; and <u>you have come to need milk and not solid food. For everyone who partakes only of milk is unskilled in the word of righteousness, for he is a babe. But solid food belongs to those who are of full age,</u> that is, those who by reason of use have their senses exercised to discern both good and evil.
Hebrews 5:12-14 (NKJV)

AND

THE LIGHT

SHINETH

IN DARKNESS

It is evident from the above scriptures that Christians can be immature and not able to understand the deeper meanings and revelations of the Bible.

MATURITY REQUIRED

Paul told the Hebrew church, we have much to say, however it is hard to communicate it all to you, since your growth in Christ has not matured. He says that everyone who uses milk is unskillful in the Word of God. Solid food belongs to them who have been walking in faith, to those who through experience and by exercising their faith have grown in their ability to discern that which is good from that which is evil.

JOURNEY REQUIREMENTS

The next few chapters are about the journey the Holy Spirit led me on. A journey that changed my viewpoint from one that believed the Bible condemned homosexual marriage to one that believes the Bible actually affirms it. It is not a journey that requires one to be a Bible scholar or be highly intelligent to take. The main requirement to reach the destination is a humble heart filled with the love of Jesus Christ. And for those who are not Christians a humble heart filled with perfect love, or put another way - loving your neighbor *as* you love yourself.

AND THE

DARKNESS

COMPREHENDED

IT NOT

4

LOOKING ON THE SURFACE

As was mentioned above, on the surface it appears that the Bible condemns homosexual marriage. This chapter will take a look at the main scriptures that Christians who condemn homosexual marriage give reference to in justifying their position.

LEVITICUS 18:21-23

Probably the most quoted scripture is Lev 18:21-23: *"Thou shalt not lie with mankind, as with womankind: it is abomination."(KJV)*

LEVITICUS 20:13

It is repeated in the 20th chapter, verse 13: *"If a man also lie with mankind, as he lieth with a woman, both of them have committed an abomination: they shall surely be put to death; their blood shall be upon them."(KJV)*

IT IS WRITTEN

THE

TRUE LIGHT

JOHN 1:9 (NET)

ROMANS 1:24-27

In the New Testament we have Romans 1:24-27:

"Therefore God also gave them up to uncleanness, in the lusts of their hearts, to dishonor their bodies among themselves, who exchanged the truth of God for the lie, and worshiped and served the creature rather than the Creator, who is blessed forever. Amen.

For this reason God gave them up to vile passions. For even their women exchanged the natural use for what is against nature. Likewise also the men, leaving the natural use of the woman, burned in their lust for one another, men with men committing what is shameful, and receiving in themselves the penalty of their error which was due." (NKJV)

HEBREWS 13:4

Hebrews chapter 13 verse 4 says this:

"Marriage is honorable among all, and the bed undefiled; but fornicators and adulterers God will judge." (NKJV)

1 CORINTHIAN 6:9-10

1st Corinthians chapter 6 verses 9-10 reads as follows:

"Know ye not that the unrighteous shall not inherit the kingdom of God? Be not deceived: neither fornicators, nor idolaters, nor adulterers, nor effeminate, nor abusers of themselves with mankind, nor thieves, nor

WHO

GIVES LIGHT

TO

EVERYONE

covetous, nor drunkards, nor revilers, nor extortioners, shall inherit the kingdom of God." (KJV)

From these scriptures, it is very understandable why many Christians, who believe the Bible is the inspired Word of God, believe that homosexual marriage is sin. I was in this group for most of my adult life.

Understanding the Bible Correctly

I still definitely believe the Bible is 100% correct, more so than ever. However I do not believe the Bible condemns homosexual marriage. The challenge is in interpreting the Bible and understanding it correctly. Does it require a highly intelligent mind to understand the Bible on a deeper level? According to Jesus and the Bible, these things are hidden from the wise and intelligent. It is not with our mental competence and intelligence that give us the ability to correctly discern the deeper things of the Bible.

Jesus expressed this when he said:
"Jesus answered and said, "I thank You, Father, Lord of heaven and earth, that You have hidden these things from the wise and prudent and have revealed them to babes." Mat 11:25 (NKJV)

In the following chapters we will go on a journey to explore the above scriptures and others on a deeper level.

WAS COMING

INTO

THE WORLD

KEY FOR CORRECT UNDERSTANDING

However, I strongly encourage you not to depend solely on the following chapters or your intellect. The absolute best, and in fact the only way, to correctly discern and interpret the Bible is with a pure heart.

God in his infinite wisdom has set safeguards to keep the proud in the dark. I am not saying to throw your intellect out. But I am saying that it takes more than intellect to see, understand, and truly discern God's Word, especially on a deeper level. The less pride there is in your heart, the deeper your understanding of Jesus and the Bible will be.

Jesus expresses this when He said:
Blessed are the pure in heart, For they shall see God.
Matthew 5:8 (NKJV)

HE

WAS IN

THE WORLD

5

AN ALARM!
CONFLICTING WITNESSES

The start of what led me to search deeper into the scriptures was that still small voice and a sense in my spirit that something was not lining up right. Typically what gives me maximum confidence is when my intellect, the Bible, and the still small voice all line up and agree.

SIN LEADS TO MORE AND GREATER SIN

It is abundantly clear from observation, experience, and the Bible that sin puts people into ever increasing bondage the more a person practices it. Thus it made complete sense to me how heterosexual lust could lead into homosexual lust. There are many examples in real life and the Bible where addicts that are in bondage to a vice or sin degenerate from one level to the next.

AND

THE WORLD

WAS

CREATED

BY HIM

RED FLAG WARNING

However what threw up a red flag for me was hearing so many testimonies of people declaring that they were born gay. If that was truly the case, I knew that was a different situation entirely. This was the first flag that came up and which caused to me to have a desire to examine the Bible deeper on what it said about homosexual sex and homosexual marriage.

BUT

THE WORLD

DID NOT

RECOGNIZE

HIM

6

THE EXPERTS ARE NOT ALWAYS THE EXPERTS

Well, if it is true that God and the Bible do not condemn homosexual marriage, how could so many prominent Christian leaders be wrong on the issue of homosexual marriage?

As much as I hate to think that prominent Christian leaders could be wrong on anything, it is very clear that they do get issues and doctrine wrong. Consider the following:

Respected Christian leaders are disagreeing and have always disagreed about many issues. They all can not be correct. So obviously some are definitely wrong.

HE

CAME TO THAT

WHICH WAS

HIS OWN

PHARISEES WERE SPIRITUALLY BLIND

Remember the Pharisees; they were the experts on Old Testament Scripture and the respected religious leaders of their time. Even though the Scriptures clearly told of Jesus coming as a suffering servant, they didn't understand or recognize Jesus when he came. This was true even after all the amazing miracles that Jesus did.

APOSTLES DISAGREED

The apostles and elders of the early church didn't always agree. (Acts 15:7) They resolved their differences by prayer, being open minded, and utilizing the Word of God as the foundation for their decisions.

EVERYDAY ORDINARY PEOPLE
WERE THE ONES WHO RECOGNIZED JESUS

A common everyday layperson, Peter, who was a fisherman, and other ordinary people like him, did recognize Jesus as the Jewish Messiah. In fact, it is interesting to note that Peter and the apostles had an awareness and sense that Jesus was the coming Jewish messiah even before Jesus did any major miracles.

BUT

HIS OWN

DID NOT

RECEIVE

HIM

IT DOESN'T FOLLOW THAT
BEING CORRECT ON SOME ISSUES
MEANS BEING CORRECT ON ALL ISSUES

While good Christian leaders can be right on many issues, it doesn't mean that they are right on all issues. In fact it is assured that they are not, due to the many disagreements between them. So, while I respect, listen to, and have learned a great deal from respected Christian leaders, it is clear that they could very easily be wrong on their stance on homosexual marriage.

YET

TO ALL

WHO RECEIVED

HIM

TO THOSE WHO

BELIEVED

IN HIS NAME

JOHN 1:12 (NIV)

7

EXAMINING OUR HEARTS AND MOTIVES

If our goal is that we want to correctly understand and interpret the Bible in regards to this issue, wouldn't it be wise or beneficial to ask ourselves and explore why Peter recognized Jesus, but the Pharisees and many Jews did not?

If you answered yes, continue reading. If you answered no, read chapters 5, 6, & 7 in the book of Matthew and write the following 500 times on a sheet of paper, "*I will be humble and open-minded.*" Then re-read and answer the question one more time.

Just kidding about the assignment for the no answer ☺. Though if you are truly living your life in accordance with Matthew 5, 6, & 7 you can skip this chapter.

HE GAVE

THE RIGHT

TO BECOME

CHILDREN

OF GOD

PHARISEES & THE DISCIPLES

From hindsight it is easy to see that the Pharisees were mainly focused on themselves. On the other hand Peter and those that followed Jesus were much more humble, were not self-righteous, were willing to repent, were open minded, and had genuine care and concern for others.

QUESTIONS

So here are some questions we should ask ourselves. Do we really care about people who are homosexual? Or, are we mainly concerned about protecting ourselves, family, and friends? Do we have the love of Jesus and love our enemies as we love ourselves? Or, do we mainly reserve our best love for those that love us and are in our circle of friends and family? Jesus said there was no reward for those who love this way. Jesus stated that even sinners love those that love them. That is worth repeating. Jesus said there is *no reward* for loving our families. (Matthew 5:46) Sounds a little extreme doesn't it?

JESUS' STANDARD

How can one truly love to Jesus' standard? It does seem a little unrealistic, impractical, and impossible to do. I assure you though that Jesus meant just that. God is perfect. (Matthew 5:48) God's love is perfect.

CHILDREN

NOT BORN

BY HUMAN PARENTS

OR BY

HUMAN DESIRE

OR A

HUSBANDS DECISION

BUT BY

GOD

PERFECT LOVE

Perfect love is unconditional. God and Jesus have perfect love for you, for me, and for everyone. In fact, Jesus loves you AS he loves himself. That statement should take your breath away. The creator of all loves me AS he loves himself. (Something to stop and think about)

THE ONLY QUESTION

God's love and Jesus' love for us is not based on what you or I do or don't do. There is no question that God and Jesus loves us. The only question is whether <u>we</u> love God and *whether we will choose* to love as He loves.

WHAT IS SIN?

Jesus is the only person who has ever lived that never once in thought or deed, loved anyone (even his enemies and those who were far off in distance or time) less than he loved himself. How do I know that? It is simple. According to God's standard, *anytime we love anyone less than we love ourselves, it is sin.* (Matthew 22:39) And Jesus never once sinned, though he was tempted as we are. (Again something to stop and think about)

NOW

THE WORD

BECAME FLESH

AND TOOK UP

RESIDENCE

AMONG US

JOHN 1:14 (NET)

WHY HEAVEN IS SO GREAT

What makes heaven so great and perfect is that everyone there has God's perfect love nature. Think about living in a place where *absolutely everyone* truly *loves you AS they love themselves*. Our human nature that we are born with falls so short of God's perfect love standard that it is impossible for us to live there as we are. The Bible says our righteousness is as filthy rags. (Isaiah 64:6)

IMPERFECT LOVE

We learn from the Bible that we are all born with an inherited selfish sin nature. This is also verified when we look inside of ourselves. We like to love some people a little more or a little less than ourselves. It is the much more comfortable way to live in this world. Satan is the master of living and loving this way. That is why he is called the Prince of this world. If we justify loving ourselves and our families a little more than we love others, how can we complain when those in power choose to love themselves more than they love us? We are doing the same thing.

PERFECT LOVE MUST BE #1 DESIRE

Jesus said that if we want anything more than Him (or put another way, if we want anything more than loving everyone perfectly) we are not worthy of Him. In other

WE

SAW HIS GLORY,

THE GLORY OF THE

ONE AND ONLY,

words our choice to love imperfectly makes us unworthy of God's gift of eternal life. Putting anything before the perfect love of God spots us out as *persons of free will* who have decided to put something else (an idol) over God's perfect love.

NO OTHER CHOICE POSSIBLE

So while this new perfect love nature is a gift, unless we make Jesus (or in other words we choose to love perfectly as He does) our number one priority, we can not and will not obtain or receive it. By choosing anything else besides the perfect love of Jesus negates what perfect love in essence is. It is like wanting to have a faithful marriage but also wanting to cheat too. It is impossible to have both. A choice and decision determines which one we will have.

PRIORITY ILLUSTRATION

Here is an illustration of loving something (in this case family) more than we love Jesus. In our eyes there may seem to be little difference between the following two groups of people:

Group A - People who have made the perfect love of God as their *number one* priority, and their family as their *second* priority.

FULL OF

GRACE AND TRUTH,

WHO CAME FROM

THE FATHER

Group B - People who have made love for their family as their *number one* priority and the perfect love of God as their *second* priority.

DIFFERENCE BETWEEN NIGHT AND DAY

However in God's eyes the difference between these two groups of people is like the difference between night and day. The Bible says to examine our hearts to make sure we do not have any idols (and one of the most tempting being family) ahead of God's perfect love and God himself.

NOT SAYING TO "NOT" LOVE FAMILY

Please note that Jesus is **not** saying: *"don't love our families."* We are to love our families AS we love ourselves. The sin comes when we choose to love our families (or any other idol) more than we love someone else (even our enemies). We must choose to love like God the Father and Jesus does in order to have eternal life in God's family. Where would we be if God and Jesus did not love us perfectly?

CAN NOT OR WILL NOT?

I can hear many out there saying: *"I can not do that"* or *"I am not going to do that."* This may feel right and it may seem like the right thing to say, (Proverbs 16:25)

IT IS WRITTEN

FOR THE

LAW

WAS GIVEN

BY

MOSES

but in actuality what they are saying is: "*I **will** not do that*" and "*I **choose** not to do that*." All of us have been given the power to freely choose if we want to do this or not. Each of us can do this. Each of us has the ability to make this choice, and each of us is 100% totally accountable for the choice we make.

TRULY LOVING OUR FAMILIES

In actuality, the only way to <u>*truly love our families*</u> is if we put God's perfect love first and foremost and encourage our families and friends to do the same. When we choose to love imperfectly and love our families a little more than others, <u>the bottom line is we are really just loving ourselves</u>. This will be easy to understand and quite evident on judgment day. God sees perfectly and will shine light on all of our iniquities and deceptions.

ANY IDOL MAKES US UNWORTHY

Of course one could put any other idol in the place of family in the above illustration and the outcome or conclusion would be identical. Whether it be money, fame, sensual pleasures, pride, ego, or whatever desire, person, place, or thing that has a higher priority than Jesus would render us unable and unworthy to receive the gift of being a person of perfect love.

BUT

GRACE AND TRUTH

CAME BY

JESUS CHRIST

When Love is Sin

The reason I used family in the illustration is because family is probably the most difficult to die to or in other words to put in subjection to perfect love. It is also the idol that can appear to look so good, holy, and loving while in actuality it is not. When one has family as an idol, ones selfishness and sin is very deceiving to both the doer and the observer. (Note: loving one's family is a good thing, the sin and evil comes when loving family takes a higher priority over loving perfectly.)

Demonstration by Jesus

Jesus demonstrated living and loving this way. Why would Jesus leave heaven, become one of us, and live his life the way he did? The only *motive* that makes sense is that he loves us as he loves himself. The *reason* he came was to make a way for us to be part of God's family and to save us from the consequences of our sins and our inherited sinful nature. If God, <u>The Creator of Heaven and Earth and All That is Therein,</u> is willing to humble himself and love like that, **who am I not to**.

IS THIS FAIR?

Is this fair? No, not in any way. Why should Jesus suffer and pay the punishment for the wrongs we have done and continue to do? Why would Jesus freely choose to pay for our transgressions? Again there is only one motive that makes sense. Jesus truly loves us AS he loves himself. Why? That is the very essence of what God's perfect love is, and makes God who He is. It is God's perfect love that makes God so indescribably great and truly worthy of all the praise of His creation!

WHERE WOULD WE BE IF
GOD'S LOVE FOR US WAS NOT PERFECT?

If we are ever tempted to wonder whether Jesus is worthy of all our praise, glory, and honor, we should just stop and ask ourselves: Where would we be if God was not a God of perfect love and Jesus did not love us perfectly? Think about how much smarter, greater, and more powerful Jesus is than us. Yet *Jesus humbles himself to love us AS He loves himself*. He has not just done it once or a few times but is continuously doing it, minute by minute, day by day, never wavering from it. He is loving you perfectly (*AS he loves himself*) that way *right now*. We can be confident He will continue to do so forever throughout eternity.

HEREIN

IS OUR LOVE

MADE PERFECT

Sensing God's Presence

If you take time to stop, thank, and give Him praise, you will find out a secret...He inhabits the praises of His children. (Psalm 22:3) It is where you will sense his presence more so than any other way. The degree we have a desire to Praise God is relative to the degree our hearts are pure and free of the deceptions of sin and selfishness.

Joy Everlasting

The joy one experiences on the inside when one first realizes and personally experiences the reality of the perfect love of God is off the charts and never goes away, even in tough times.

Why It Is Available

The ability and potential for us to walk in perfect love has been made available to us by Jesus' life and what He did on the cross to atone for our sins.

Receiving a Perfect Love Nature

If we repent of our sins (or put another way, repent of loving imperfectly or loving some people more or less than others) and receive Jesus as Lord of our life, two things will happen. 1) Our sins will be forgiven and atoned for (made possible & justifiable as a result of Jesus' crucifixion). And 2) We will receive a perfect

THAT WE MAY HAVE

BOLDNESS

IN THE DAY OF

JUDGMENT

1 JOHN 4:17 (KJV)

love nature like unto Jesus'. We may not look different on the outside, but on the inside we will have a brand new nature. In essence, on the inside we become a brand new person. (2 Corinthians 5:17)

OUR CHOICE
LEADS TO
GOD'S UNSPEAKABLE GIFT
OF HIS RIGHTEOUSNESS
AND PERFECT LOVE NATURE
WHICH
ALLOWS US TO BE
CITIZENS OF HEAVEN
&
MEMBERS OF
GOD'S ETERNAL FAMILY

UNSPEAKABLE GIFT

This unspeakable gift (which we all have the opportunity to receive by simply renouncing our selfish nature and receiving Jesus' perfect love nature) allows us to live in heaven as part of God's

BECAUSE AS

HE IS,

SO ARE WE

IN THIS WORLD

1 JOHN 4:17 (KJV)

family. Because we have freely chosen to make Jesus our Lord, Jesus is able to make restitution for our sins and God can justly attribute Jesus' righteousness to us. (2 Corinthians 5:21).

OLD NATURE STILL PRESENT IN PART

It is also helpful to understand that when we receive this new perfect love nature, our old selfish desires and temptations do not just automatically go away. We will still have some temptations to love imperfectly and be selfish to a degree (but usually to a much lesser degree). Our new nature though will give us a desire to resist our selfish temptations and there is also strength available to overcome them. What we choose to yield ourselves to (whether temptations to be selfish and love imperfectly, or to be obedient to what our new perfect love nature is guiding us to do) will determine which nature (our old or new) will grow stronger.

VICTORY IN PARTNERSHIP

One of my favorite sayings is one that my mother used to say: *"Do your best and God will take care of the rest."* This is not a verse in the Bible but it is clearly a biblical principal. If we **make our choice and do our best**, God will take care of the rest.

FREE WILL AND LOVE

To truly have the ability to be able to love means we have to have <u>free</u> <u>will</u> and be able to *freely* choose. God could force us to act loving but that would not be real or actual love.

TWO PURPOSES FOR OUR LIVES

It is apparent from the Bible that one of the purposes of our lives in this world is to *freely choose our eternal destiny.* Another purpose of God for giving us human life in this world is to give us some time to be convicted of our sin and some time to repent. The Bible implies that what we choose in this world is what we would always choose no matter how many chances God would give us.

WE CHOOSE FOR ETERNITY

The Bible tells us that our decision (whether or not we give our lives in exchange for God's unspeakable gift) is *eternal.* At some point in our life we cross a line and what we have decided upon and have chosen is set in stone and will be for all eternity. This is why the Bible encourages us that if today we hear His voice to harden not our hearts. (Hebrews 3:7,8)

THERE IS NO FEAR

IN

LOVE

Why Mention Hell?

I only mention the subject of hell because the Bible tells us that there are some who will only turn away from their imperfect love and sin (and escape the eternal punishment that their sin brings) because of fear. (Jude 1:23) Many things about life are over our heads for us to understand. We are in fact not meant to, or expected to fully understand the why's of eternal judgment at this point in our lives. There is nothing that sounds worse to me than an eternity in hell. So I encourage everyone with all that I am to choose eternal life made available by the perfect love of God and Jesus Christ. I can assure you that God wants absolutely no one to go there.

How Can Hell Be Real With a God of Perfect Love?

Maybe the best answer for the above question is because God *IS* a God of Perfect Love. There is no other option for a God of perfect love and perfect righteousness. For many (myself included) the concept of an eternal hell is too much for me to get my mind around and get a grasp of how this could be possible with a perfectly loving God in control. I believe it is so though because the Bible and Jesus clearly say that it is a reality. I can certainly understand punishing evil. One thing I am absolutely quite confident about is that God

BUT

PERFECT LOVE

CASTS OUT

FEAR

1 JOHN 4:18 (NKJV)

is perfectly good and holy. If hell is as it is described to be, I am sure that God has good justifications for why it is as it is. As we continue to grow in our knowledge and understanding at some point we will most likely gain a better understanding of why hell is as it is. In this life, the Bible seems to indicate that it is sufficient for us to trust that God is loving, merciful, and righteous and accept it by faith.

GOD SENDS NO ONE TO HELL

The people who claim that a loving God would not send anyone to an eternal hell are correct. God sends no one to hell. Those who go there according to the Bible have chosen to send themselves there. Going to hell is 100% the consequence a person's choice to reject the opportunity to repent and receive the gift of eternal life. God has absolutely no control over a person's choice. If He did we would not have free will. And if we did not have free will we would not have the ability to love.

THE INTEGRITY OF THE BIBLE

The people who claim that the Bible has been changed or manipulated by man are people who have rejected its message to repent, believe, and receive eternal life. The integrity of the Bible manuscripts are without question impeccable to those who are willing to do

BECAUSE

FEAR

INVOLVES

TORMENT

their homework and look at the manuscript evidence. Those making such claims are going off hearsay and have done no research or study themselves. They are living in ignorance and darkness.

Only One Thing to Fear

As I said in a previous chapter the only thing we have to fear is that which God has absolutely no control over. And the only thing that God has absolutely no control over is *our free will*, which we are, rightfully so, totally responsible for. So when we freely choose the sinful behavior of imperfect love when we have the clear option of choosing God's perfect love, we are totally responsible for the consequences. There is absolutely nothing God can do. God has absolutely no control over our choice. God is holy and has no choice but to judge righteously. God is merciful and longsuffering but there is a limit. There has to be if God is truly loving and righteous. If you are hearing God calling you, humble yourself and receive forgiveness and life eternal right now where you are.

Challenging God

For a human being (who has been created by God) to think that they can challenge God on his morality, on hell, or any other moral issue, displays the height of foolishness and pride. God is merciful and loving but

BUT

HE WHO FEARS

HAS NOT BEEN MADE

PERFECT IN LOVE

1 JOHN 4:18 (NKJV)

He is also perfect in righteousness. The Bible clearly teaches that no wrong or injustice will go without a fair judgment. Who are we to think that (with our low mental capacity, understanding, and our meager abilities) we know better than God?

SIN DECEIVES

Many sins deceive the doer into believing they are not sinning or that the sin is actually good. Take the Muslim extremists who flew their planes in the World Trade Center towers. Their sin deceived them into thinking that they were doing God's work and would be rewarded in the next life.

WE MAY BE SINNING
AND NOT KNOW IT

That example should send up a warning flag to us. Just because we do not think that we are sinning does not mean we are not. If the Muslim extremists can be deceived in thinking that such an atrocious act is good, how much more should we be concerned of being deceived by less outwardly vile sins. We should always be asking the Holy Spirit to examine our hearts and reveal any wicked and deceptive ways in us. (Psalms 139:23) This is proved over and over in our own lives when increased maturity exposes our youthful sins that we had been totally blind too, many

WE LOVE

BECAUSE

HE LOVED US

FIRST

of which we also thought were acts of love and goodness. We should always be vigilant and concerned to the possibility that we may be committing sins right now that we are unaware of.

FORGIVENESS IS ESSENTIAL

God will not hold us accountable for the wrongs that others do. He will hold us accountable for all the wrongs that we do though. If we want God to forgive us (our sins of omission as well as our sins of commission) then we need to forgive those who have wronged us. Otherwise God will not forgive us for our sins. (Matthew 6:15)

RELIGION – GOOD OR BAD

Some say that religion should be banned. Look at the evil it has done. This too is said by people who have not yet been convicted and repented of their imperfect love nature. Much bad has been done in the name of religions both Christian and non-Christian. However much good has also been done in the name of religion. The bottom line however is that without a new nature made available by Jesus Christ no one can be truly good. To the extent that other religions follow Christ's teachings, they are good. To the extent that other religions do not follow Christ's teachings, they are not good and lead people astray from the truth.

IF SOMEONE SAYS,

"I LOVE GOD,"

1 JOHN 4:20 (NKJV)

COMMON ERRORS OF RELIGION

One teaching that most other religions get wrong is that we can be good on our own and our good works can earn us entrance into heaven. They are totally ignorant that it is only by the gift of a new nature and the perfect righteousness of Jesus Christ can we have any hope of being part of God's family in heaven. The second most important understanding that other religions and even many Christian churches are ignorant of is: that in order to receive this new nature and the gift of the righteousness of Jesus Christ, a person can not have any idols above God's perfect love (which has been made available to us by Jesus Christ). God's perfect love has to be a person's number one priority and motivation.

CAN A HINDU BE A CHRISTIAN UNAWARES?

There are many in the world who have never heard the gospel of Jesus Christ but they have nevertheless naturally and instinctively on their own have died to themselves and have committed to living their lives in perfect love. In God's eyes these are true Christians even though they are ignorant of who Jesus is and are unaware that they have been born anew with a new nature of God's perfect love. John says that *everyone* that has perfect love has been born again and knows God. (1 John 4:7)

AND

HATES

HIS BROTHER

Many Christians have a false hope

In the opposite manner there are many who are life long Christians who have heard about and know the message of the Gospel of Jesus Christ but haven't taken it to heart or fully understood it. They believe that they are Christian but in actuality they have a false hope. The Jesus that they think they know is a Jesus of imperfect love. (1 John 4:8) The real Jesus undoubtedly at some point in their life knocked on their heart but they rejected him (because of peer pressure, inconvenience, selfishness, the glitter of this world, family, etc.). Or, maybe the real Jesus has not yet revealed himself to them. There is always no better time - for someone to ask Jesus to make himself and his perfect love personally real and for one to make the decision to give their life in exchange for an eternity of perfect love - than now.

No Better Time - No Better Place

Is life really worth living without perfect love? Isn't perfect love the only solution to the world's problems? What is better than being a person of "perfect love" and soon to be living in a world of perfect love? Jesus calls out to all who are heavily burdened. He pledges to assist us with the load and to give us rest. (Matthew 11:28-30) To anyone who has not yet repented and received Jesus Christ as Lord of their lives, trust God to do His part. You will be in God's hands and no one

HE

IS A

LIAR

will be able to pluck you out of them. (John 10:29) There is no safer place.

WE ARE BEING TESTED AND GIVEN AN OPPPORTUNITY AND TIME TO REPENT

God puts us in situations to test us and to expose what we will choose. Those situations reveal the quality of person that we have chosen to be. God is all merciful and understands our weakness and gives us some time and space to repent and choose differently. However God, being perfect, is also perfect in righteousness and will deal justly with all wrong in due time. All the wrongs that have been committed against us and all of the wrongs that we have committed will be accounted for and dealt with justly and fairly according to God's standards. The guilty will not go unpunished. (Proverbs 11:21)

WRITTEN FOR THE BRIDE

This book contains perspectives & revelations that undoubtedly many will find revolutionary and radical. They will find fault with them. Some will call the book blasphemous. I have written what I felt called to write. I believe the Bride of Christ will hear and take these teachings to heart. I encourage everyone to read their Bible and seek God to verify these things for

FOR

HE WHO DOES

NOT LOVE

HIS BROTHER

WHOM

HE HAS SEEN

themselves. I do not claim to be spiritually above any other person. These topics however are areas that I believe that God has given me special understanding and insight on. The writing of this book is a part of what God has raised me up, trained me, and called me to do.

PURPOSE OF BOOK

The purpose of this book is to illuminate and open up biblical truths. This book supports and affirms the Bible as the inspired Word of God. It endeavors only to shine light on what is already in the scriptures and to assist in making them clearer and more understandable. Everything said in this book is Bible based. This book in no way disagrees with or contradicts the Bible. There is no claim of any new revelations not already written about in the Bible.

THE MOST IMPORTANT CHAPTER

This chapter turned out to be the longest. It turned out that way probably for the most part because it is the most important. Without having an authentic new birth experience, it will be impossible to understand not only the next chapter but any of the deeper things in the Word of God. Most importantly though without being born anew (made available to us by Jesus Christ) one cannot truly be part of God's eternal family.

HOW CAN HE

LOVE GOD

WHOM HE HAS

NOT SEEN?

1 JOHN 4:20 (NKJV)

IN SUMMARY

If you are Christian and you look inside of yourself and do not find this perfect love nature, then you will likely find it difficult to understand or agree with what the following chapters in this book are saying.

If on the other hand you look inside of yourself and you do find in your heart a desire to love others perfectly, not just your family and friends, but also your enemies; such as, loving them truly AS you love yourself, then you will likely not find it too difficult or hard to understand and agree with the following chapters.

AND THIS

COMMANDMENT

WE HAVE FROM

HIM

8

LOOKING AND UNDERSTANDING ON A DEEPER LEVEL

I once thought as most conservative Christians that the Bible condemned everything homosexual. As I said previously something was not lining up with that perspective and caused me to have a question mark.

The following scripture seems very straight forward which is from the Old Testament.
Thou shalt not lie with mankind, as with womankind: it is abomination. Leviticus 18:22 (KJV)

Another Old Testament commandment says:
"Thou shall not eat any abominable thing." Deuteronomy 14:3 (KJV)

THAT HE

WHO LOVES

GOD

MUST LOVE

HIS BROTHER

ALSO

1 JOHN 4:21 (NKJV)

A DIFFERENCE BETWEEN
OLD AND NEW TESTAMENTS

Eating pork is abominable according to Old Testament scripture. However the Church or at least a significant part of the mainstream Christian church today says that this abominable thing of eating pork has been changed and it is quite acceptable and OK for Christians to eat pork today. This is one example among many that there is a difference between the law of the Old Testament and the grace of the New Testament.

Here is another example.
"Work shall be done for six days, but the seventh is the Sabbath of rest, holy to the LORD. Whoever does any work on the Sabbath day, he shall surely be put to death." Exodus 31:15 (NKJV)

This is another case where what the Old Testament scripture clearly states (the death penalty for working on Sunday) has been superceded by grace that came through the New Testament and Jesus Christ.

LAW AND GRACE

An open-minded, Bible-believing Christian would then have to acknowledge the possibility that Leviticus 18:22, like Exodus 31:15, could also be null and void under the New Testament. Christians that have studied

to show themselves approved should have a good understanding of the differences between Law and Grace. This leads us to conclude that Leviticus 18:22 could possibly also be one of those scriptures that doesn't get an exact carry over from the Old Testament to the New Testament.

NOT SAYING PERVERTED SEX IS NOT SIN

At this point I believe it is important to keep in mind what this book is endeavoring to show. I am not saying that perverse homosexual sexual activity is not sin and abominable. What I am endeavoring to show is that the Bible on a deeper level allows for and supports homosexual marriage.

MORE SCRIPTURES REQUIRED

So in conclusion from the above, I believe it is clear that one can not confidently conclude from Lev 18:22 alone that the Bible condemns homosexual marriage. Obviously there are more scriptures in the Word of God that need to be looked at. This is especially true for Christians who really care about correctly interpreting the Word of God.

OK, let's now look at some New Testament scriptures: *"Know ye not that the unrighteous shall not inherit the kingdom of God? Be not deceived: neither fornicators,*

THE FIRST

OF ALL THE

COMMANDMENTS

IS:

nor idolaters, nor adulterers, <u>nor effeminate</u>, <u>nor</u> *<u>abusers of themselves with mankind</u>, nor thieves, nor covetous, nor drunkards, nor revilers, nor extortioners, shall inherit the kingdom of God.*" 1 Cor. 6; 9-10 (KJV)

DEFINITION OF "MALAKOS"

There are people who say that "*nor effeminate, nor abusers of themselves with mankind*" in the above verses refers to homosexuals. Let's start with the word effeminate. The Greek word here is "*malakos*" whose root and basic meaning is "*soft to the touch*." The best source to gain a good understanding of its' meaning is to check if this Greek word is used anywhere else in Scripture and in what context. Well, we are very fortunate, because "*malakos*" is used in two other scriptures. (Mat 11:8 & Luke 7:25). We are also doubly fortunate because Jesus himself defines "*malakos*." Jesus himself says. "*Behold*" (and I note Jesus said Behold) they that wear "*malakos*" or soft clothing (who are they?) they are gorgeously appareled and live in luxury and in palaces.

Hear, O Israel,

the Lord our God,

the Lord

is One

So if we read 1 Cor 6:9,10 with the word *"effeminate"* translated the same way that Jesus used the word. It would read:

"Know ye not that the unrighteous shall not inherit the kingdom of God? Be not deceived: neither fornicators, nor idolaters, nor adulterers, <u>nor those who live luxurious self-indulgent life styles</u>, nor abusers of themselves with mankind, nor thieves, nor covetous, nor drunkards, nor revilers, nor extortioners, shall inherit the kingdom of God."

Anyone can translate *"malakos"* into English any way they want. That is why some translations contradict each other. That is also one reason God tells us to study the Bible ourselves. I will trust Jesus' definition other than a man's translation that can easily be influenced by culture, prejudice, or tradition. (which by the way are things the Bible warns us to watch out for)

LOOKING AT THE ORIGINAL GREEK

Well that leaves *"abusers of themselves with mankind"* the Greek word for that is *"arsenokoites"* this word is used again by Paul in his letter to Timothy in the same sort of context and list. That leaves us with utilizing the context of the word for help in translating.

AND

YOU SHALL LOVE

THE LORD

YOUR GOD

DEFINITION OF "PORNOS"

The Greek word for *"fornicators"* in the above scripture is *"pornos."* Pornos is used 10 times in the New Testament in similar context as it is in 1 Cor 6:9. It is typically translated whoremonger or fornicator in English. Another way of saying the same thing would be *"a sexually perverse heterosexual."*

DEFINITION OF "ARSENOKOITES"

From context then *"arsenokoites"* could in a similar way be translated into English as *"a sexually perverse homosexual"* Some Greek dictionaries translate the word as sodomite.

TRANSLATING 1 COR 6:9,10
WITH REFINED DEFINITIONS

So again substituting that into 1 Cor 6:9,10 we have: *"Know ye not that the unrighteous shall not inherit the kingdom of God? Be not deceived: neither sexually perverse heterosexuals, nor idolaters, nor adulterers, nor those who live luxurious self-indulgent life styles, nor sexually perverse homosexuals, nor thieves, nor covetous, nor drunkards, nor revilers, nor extortioners, shall inherit the kingdom of God."*

WITH

ALL YOUR HEART

ROMANS 1:22 TO 28

Another New Testament scripture that is quoted frequently is Romans 1:22-28:

*Professing themselves to be wise, they became fools, And changed the glory of the uncorruptible God into an image made like to corruptible man, and to birds, and fourfooted beasts, and creeping things. <u>Wherefore God also gave them up to uncleanness through the lusts of their own hearts, to dishonour their own bodies between themselves</u>: Who changed the truth of God into a lie, and worshipped and served the creature more than the Creator, who is blessed for ever. Amen. For this cause <u>God gave them up unto vile affections</u>: for even their women did change the natural use into that which is against nature: And likewise also the men, leaving the natural use of the woman, <u>burned in their **lust** one toward another</u>; men with men working that which is unseemly, and receiving in themselves that recompence of their error which was meet. And even as they did not like to retain God in their knowledge, God gave them over to a reprobate mind, to do those things which are not convenient; (KJV)*

These scriptures are clearly about God giving up *"fools who changed the truth of God into a lie"* to uncleanness through the <u>lusts of their own hearts</u>, to dishonor their own bodies between themselves.

IT IS WRITTEN

WITH

ALL YOUR SOUL

BIBLE CLEARLY CALLS LUST SIN

The Bible is abundantly clear that lust is sin and part of the kingdom of darkness. The Bible makes it clear that sexually perverse homosexuals as well as sexually perverse heterosexuals will not enter the kingdom of God.

I can see where on a superficial level that one might come away thinking these scriptures imply that anything to do with homosexuality is sin. However if one looks at these scriptures on a deeper level, what they are actually saying is that God gave up highly rebellious anti-God degenerates to sexually perverse homosexual lust. Saying that being a homosexual or anything to do with homosexuality is sin is adding to what these scriptures are saying.

AN INTRIGUING QUESTION

An intriguing question that comes up is: Why wouldn't God give up these vile lustful people to heterosexual lusting instead of giving them up to homosexual lusting? This is just speculation on my part but it is interesting and I will share it as food for thought. Possibly in God's love, mercy, and compassion, He gave them up to same-sex lust to keep the opposite gender from the consequences that would be inflicted

WITH

ALL YOUR MIND

LOOKING AND UNDERSTANDING ON A DEEPER LEVEL

upon them by unconscionable sexual degenerates. Think about man's greater physical strength and man's dominance of women in society throughout history. I won't elaborate but it sounds like something the compassionate God I know would do. God does protect us way more than we have the capacity to realize. I am sure that God has many reasons. It is not for us to always know why God does things. It is sufficient for us to know that God is good and that no evil comes from Him.

WHAT TO FEAR

The great evils in the world that would seek to harm us are not what we should be scared of. God can easily protect us from them. The only thing that has merit for us to fear is that which God has absolutely no control over. And the only that God has absolutely no control over is *our free will*, which we are, rightfully so, totally responsible for.

HEBREW 13:4

Here is also another new scripture that is quoted often: *"Marriage is honorable among all, and the bed undefiled;"* (Heb 13:4) (NKJV)

Some Christians say that allowing homosexual couples to marry would defile the institution of marriage. We

AND WITH

ALL YOUR STRENGTH

have seen that the Bible clearly condemns perverse homosexual lust and behavior. However, so far though we have not found that under the grace of the New Testament that the Bible condemns homosexual marriage.

LOOKING CLOSER AT HEBREWS 13:4

Let's take a closer look at Heb 13:4. It says that marriage is honorable. It is saying that it is the marriage that makes the (sexual) bed undefiled. In other words it is not the sexual orientation or the sex that makes the marriage honorable. It is just the opposite. It is the marriage that makes the sex or the bed undefiled.

WHAT DEFILES A MAN

If we think about it, this lines up with what Jesus said when He said that it is what comes out of the heart that defiles a man.

"For from within, out of the heart of men, proceed evil thoughts, adulteries, fornications, murders, thefts, covetousness, wickedness, deceit, lewdness, an evil eye, blasphemy, pride, foolishness. All these evil things come from within and defile a man." (Mark 7:21-23) (NKJV)

THIS IS *THE*

FIRST COMMANDMENT

The Marriage Covenant Sanctifies

The marriage covenant is a declaration of the unselfish exclusive love that the couple has in their hearts for one another. It is this unselfish and committed love for each other that sanctifies and makes pure the sex of the marriage bed. It is clearly not the sex and or the sexual orientation that makes the marriage honorable. The only way we can bring sexual orientation into Heb 13:4 is by adding our preconceived beliefs, culture, and ideology to it.

Greek word for Marriage "Gamos"

It is even more evident that Hebrews 13:4 is not talking about or referencing anything in regard to sexual orientation if we dig a little deeper. We find the Greek word for marriage in this verse is "gamos." It is used 16 times in the New Testament. In most of those occurrences it refers to the Marriage of Christ and His Bride. Obviously in this context marriage is not about sexual orientation or even sex. Also note that many that will make up the Bride of Christ will be male.

Marriage is honorable among **?**

It is also worth noting that Hebrews 13:4 says that marriage is honorable *among all*. Does *among all* mean just heterosexuals? No. Could *among all* include

AND

THE SECOND,

LIKE IT,

IS THIS:

homosexuals? Yes, all means everyone. So in actuality one could translate Hebrews 13:4 as:
"Marriage is honorable among heterosexuals and homosexuals."

BEING CAREFUL NOT TO ADD TO SCRIPTURE

Again it is worth noting that it is so easy to add to or take away from what scripture actually says, and also without realizing it, add to the scriptures our own preferences and prejudices. This is why the Bible encourages us to be diligent and seek after God and the Bible with a pure heart.

Thus we can confidently conclude that marriage is what sanctifies the bed, as opposed to the *"sexual orientation"* making the marriage honorable.

WHO TRIES TO DESTROY MARRIAGE?

If marriage is a good thing according to the Bible, let's ask ourselves a question. Who according to the Bible tries to destroy marriages and tempts people to live sexually perverse lifestyles? The Bible clearly tells us that Satan comes to kill, steal, and destroy. Do you think that it is possible that Satan might also want to deny marriage to a homosexual couple and thus encourage them to practice sexual promiscuous and

YOU

SHALL LOVE

YOUR NEIGHBOR

<u>AS</u>

YOURSELF.

perverse lifestyles? Do you also think that Satan might also take delight in making the Christian church look prudish, out of touch, and unloving? Without a doubt, the answer is an emphatic yes. Satan's fingerprints and evidence of his influence are all over this controversial topic.

BEHIND THE SCENES

Whenever two groups or people are fighting, have you ever noticed how Satan is usually involved on both sides of the argument and in actuality, inciting each side on. Satan helps each side clearly see the wrongs of the other side and makes each side blind to their own wrongs.

FORBIDDING TO MARRY

Doesn't Timothy in the Bible say that in the latter times that some shall give heed to deceiving spirits and doctrines of demons and will *forbid others from marrying*? (1Timothy 4:1-3) Could it be that Satan has deceived the mainstream Christian church to do his bidding for him? There is only one group I know that takes a stance in regards to forbidding marriage. Why would a loving person forbid something honorable to another person or group that they love? I can not think of any reason, but I can think of many reasons why Satan would. Could this doctrine of forbidding

THERE

IS NO OTHER

COMMANDMENT

GREATER

THAN THESE

MARK 12:31 (NKJV)

marriage to homosexuals be one of the doctrines of demons that 1 Timothy 4:1-3 is referring to? Could this master deceiver be pulling a big deception over on a significant part of the mainstream Christian church?

I believe the answer is clearly yes. God is raising up a bride though without spot or blemish who will be able to rightly divide the Word of God. (Ephesians 5:27)

WHY NOT MAKE IT CLEARER?

A fair question that can be asked is: If God is not against homosexual marriage, then why wouldn't He clearly say in the Bible that homosexual marriage was OK?

That is a good question. God is thousands of times smarter than all of us put together (which is actually a huge understatement). I am also sure He has many if not thousands of reasons for doing each and every one of the things that He does. I am not saying that the following is why but one thought that comes to mind is this:

Why didn't God make it abundantly clear that when the Messiah came He would first come as a suffering servant, leave the world, and then return later as a conquering king? It is clear from hindsight that God

only wanted to reveal himself to the truly humble and righteous and not to the proud and self-righteous.

So in the same way maybe God made this issue about homosexual marriage a little unclear on purpose for the same reason. In order to separate unto Himself those that are truly humble from the proud and self-righteous before His second coming.

FOR GOD

SO LOVED

THE WORLD

JOHN 3:16 (NKJV)

9

IN CONCLUSION

It is clear the Bible speaks out against all sexually perverse individuals. Are all heterosexuals sexually perverse? Are all homosexuals sexually perverse? The answer to both questions is No, definitely not.

A significant percentage of the Christian church today believes they are being persecuted for standing up for a biblical principle. Many are doing it in ignorance and are simply trusting in the teachings of their Christian leaders. The time is now though for those who love God and know Jesus to rightly divide the Word of God in regards to homosexual marriage.

BRIDAL PREPARATION

Jesus is coming soon and He is coming for a Bride that is ready for her wedding. The time is now for us to get

THAT

HE GAVE

rid of our spots and blemishes and to seek out an abundant supply of oil (the Holy Spirit). The Bible tells us when the door is shut on the wedding feast; it will be shut and not reopened to let in late comers. The Bible encourages us to be diligent for we do not know the time of His coming. (Matthew 25)

GOD HAS GIVEN US ALL AN INVITATION

Today, God the Father extends His unspeakable gift to all. Each of us can receive a new heart that is like unto Jesus' heart by repenting, believing, and receiving this gift of eternal life made available to us only through His son, Jesus Christ. It is a gift that we all are able to receive, regardless of our past.

DIVINE MARRIAGE COVENANT

The divine marriage covenant, that we have the opportunity to enter in with Jesus, can be simply expressed as follows: If we will give all we are and all we have to Him, He will give all He is and all He has to us.

THE BOTTOM LINE

The bottom line is this. If we choose perfect love first and foremost, we are in actuality choosing Jesus. We will receive Jesus' righteousness, a new heart nature of

HIS ONLY

BEGOTTEN SON

perfect love, and an eternal life in heaven. If we choose anything else, we are choosing imperfect love. We are not choosing Jesus. We will not receive a new heart nature. We will not be a true child of God and we will not live with God's family in heaven.

WITHOUT JESUS WE HAVE CHOSEN TO FEND FOR OURSELVES

If we turn Jesus down we will have freely chosen to be on our own and are accountable for who we are and for all that we have done.

MEASURING OUR LOVE FOR JESUS

Remember, when we stand before Jesus on our day of accountability, how much we love Jesus will be determined by, *how much we love the person that we love the least*, and **not** by, how much we love the person or persons that we love the most. (Matthew 25:40)

THAT

WHOEVER

BELIEVES

IN HIM

WORTHY OF ALL PRAISE, HONOR, AND GLORY

Is God the Father, Jesus, and the Holy Spirit worthy of all our praise, glory, and honor forever and ever, *or What!!!*

Amen and Hallelujah!!!

Forever and Ever!!!

SHOULD

NOT PERISH

JOHN 3:16 (NKJV)

ABOUT THE AUTHOR

William J. Meiners experienced God's love at a young age and has diligently pursued a greater understanding and close relationship with God ever since. He lives a committed and simple life-style and is very enthusiastic and excited about the future. He has degrees in both theology and mechanical engineering. He is an author and U.S. patent holder. William resides in Southern Indiana. He can be contacted at: WJMeiners@gmail.com

BUT HAVE

EVERLASTING LIFE